HISTORY

OF THE

POST OFFICE RIFLES

8TH BATTALION

CITY OF LONDON REGIMENT

1914 TO 1918

The Naval & Military Press Ltd

Published by

The Naval & Military Press Ltd
Unit 10 Ridgewood Industrial Park,
Uckfield, East Sussex,
TN22 5QE England

Tel: +44 (0) 1825 749494
Fax: +44 (0) 1825 765701

www.naval-military-press.com
www.nmarchive.com

In reprinting in facsimile from the original, any imperfections are inevitably reproduced and the quality may fall short of modern type and cartographic standards.

CONTENTS

		PAGE
I. A FOREWORD		v
II. THE LONDON TERRITORIAL IN ACTION		1
III. BATTLE HONOURS (1914 TO 1918)		4
IV. THE POST OFFICE RIFLES (1914 TO 1918)		5
1. PRELIMINARY—		
ORGANIZATION		5
THE RESERVE BATTALION		5
COMMITTEES		6
2. THE 1/8TH BATTALION—		
EARLY DAYS		6
FESTUBERT		7
LOOS		9
VIMY		11
SOMME		14
MESSINES		15
CAMBRAI		17
3. THE 2/8TH BATTALION—		
EARLY DAYS		19
BULLECOURT		20
YPRES, WURST FARM		22
YPRES, PASSCHENDAELE		25
4. THE 8TH BATTALION—		
ST. QUENTIN		27
DEFENCE OF AMIENS		29
SOMME		31
EPEHY		34
FINAL PURSUIT		35
ARMISTICE DAY		37
PERUWELZ		37
V. SPECIAL ORDER (NOVEMBER 11TH, 1918)		39
VI. SUMMARY OF CASUALTIES		40
VII. LIST OF HONOURS		41

I

A FOREWORD

THIS is not intended to be an official history of the Post Office Rifles during the Great War. Hurriedly compiled during the few intervals of leisure permitted to a Battalion Commander in a theatre of war, it is bound to be incomplete, probably incorrect in many details, and certainly incapable of doing justice to the achievements of the Regiment.

The original idea of bringing out a peace magazine to be published in Belgium has gradually developed, until it now assumes its present form, and is published rather as a souvenir or sketch to remind the fighting man of some glorious and crowded hours of life, than as a regimental record to be handed down to posterity.

The recollections of many officers and men have been supplemented by notebooks, orders, and reports, and the lists of casualties and honours are taken from official sources. To all who have so generously assisted the thanks of the compiler are due.

No one who has not actually taken part with the fighting infantry can realize the grim reality of " going over the top "— the agony of suspense, the strained nerves, the tense moments of uncertainty, the superhuman endurance, and the glory of success, all belong to the fighting man, and to him alone. The compiler, who is not a Territorial, but whose privilege it has been to command the Post Office Rifles in France, desires to offer these pages as a tribute to the splendid fighting qualities of his Territorial comrades, naming by way of dedication one who has given many years and much honour to the Post Office Rifles, Brigadier-General A. Maxwell, C.M.G., D.S.O., Commanding the 174th Infantry Brigade.

BELGIUM,
 February, 1919.

II

THE LONDON TERRITORIAL IN ACTION

An Appreciation by Lieutenant-Colonel A. D. Derviche-Jones, D.S.O., M.C. (King's Own Royal Lancaster Regiment), Commanding 8th Battalion The City of London Regiment (Post Office Rifles).

The foundation of all sound training is that every man should understand what he has to do, how to do it, and why he has to do it, and of these the "why and wherefore" is the paramount influence in the training of the Londoner, and differentiates him most from other classes of soldier.

<small>Training.</small>

Born and bred in a large city, where his wits have been sharpened from his earliest days by the strenuous competition for existence, he is brimful of common sense, and quick to learn and to respond to anything which appeals to his intelligence. The drill-sergeant's monologue of interminable detail bores him to tears; he requires to be shown how to hold his rifle, and why he has to hold it in this way or that; once this is explained to him intelligently, he has got it, and rarely forgets. This applies with even greater force to his tactical training. Let him have a clear reason for any job that he is called upon to carry out, and why it has to be done in a particular way, and he can be trained for any enterprise, however complicated, in a very short space of time.

After a particularly severe fight in the Ypres Salient, in which this Battalion had been highly successful, a General asked a rifleman, selected purely by haphazard, whether he had found the job a difficult one. The reply was: "'Twas like shelling peas, sir; we all knew where to go and how to get there, and we just went." The barrel of this man's rifle had been broken by a Boche bullet, the butt smashed over a Boche head, and three Boches had been knocked down by his fists, before he got to the final objective. To him these were merely the trivial and necessary incidents of a journey to a particular spot which he had been taught to recognize and understood as his final objective. He and his comrades knew why it was incumbent on them to reach this particular place, and understood why they had to adopt certain formations and carry out certain manœuvres in order to get there. They were prepared for any emergency: to come to close quarters with the Boche *en route* was merely a piece of unexpected sport, but not a difficulty worth mentioning to a General.

WORK. A deal of nonsense has been spoken about the inability of the London Territorial to do effectively the manual labour involved in digging and the repair of trenches. A General once said to me: " It's no good expecting the Londoner to do this sort of work; he is not a miner or agricultural labourer—he is too intelligent to dig !" After two years with London Territorials, I beg leave to say that he is quite as capable and will carry out as good manual labour as any other soldier, provided that he is properly handled.

One cannot by merely putting a rifle into a man's hand make him a good shot or a good soldier, nor can one expect any man to become an expert sapper by handing him a spade or a pick; in both cases he must be trained for his job. If he is told why the work must be done, and how to use his spade, his pick, and his muscles; if his interest is aroused in the work (this can be done competitively); if his labour is properly organized, so as to avoid the inconceivable delays in getting to work; if he or his platoon is given a piece job, and if his comfort is properly attended to—such as hot soup on returning from a night job, etc.—the London Territorial will turn out as good work as any other soldier, and has actually and generally done so.

DISCIPLINE. The highest form of discipline depends on understanding. The rigid and automatic discipline of the Boches would not be suitable to, or bring out the best and most useful qualities of the Londoner, who is, however, always ready to admit that discipline, in the sense that it engenders collective courage in a unit, is essential to the success of the unit and the individuals composing it, and is therefore to be encouraged. He realizes that his well-being as a soldier depends on organization, and that without discipline there can be no real organization; therefore he responds to discipline as a necessary factor for his safety, his comfort, and his usefulness as a fighting man. It is his intelligence and his common sense that make him a disciplined soldier. To be effective, discipline must be sensibly and tactfully administered. At a dinner given soon after the declaration of Armistice by the Mayor of an outpost village in Belgium, which had been for four years a Boche training-centre, one of the speakers said: " I like your English discipline. The discipline of the Boches is that of a bully; yours is that of the father of a family."

The cases of serious offences during my long association with the Londoners in France can be numbered on the fingers of one hand, while petty offences are almost unknown.

He is by nature self-reliant and an individualist, and will contrive to make himself comfortable in all weathers and all places, without waiting for orders or assistance from Headquarters. Always cheerful even under the most depressing circumstances, he will say, with a broad grin, how many Boches he has prodded that day with his bayonet, or refer to his outpost shell-hole, half-filled with mud and slime, as " a boarding-house at Southend-on-Sea." A surprising factor to me has been his extraordinary grit and powers of endurance, and especially in the case of the youngsters sent out as reinforcements after the retreat of March, 1918. The defence of Amiens in April, 1918, and the vital necessity of holding old and preparing new positions in May, June, and July of that year, gave no time for the training of these reinforcements for an offensive. Owing to heavy casualties, the officer personnel had undergone frequent changes, and was for the most part inexperienced. It was sheer grit and endurance that carried these youngsters through the exceptionally heavy fighting on the Somme in August and September, 1918, where the ground was disputed inch by inch by trained enemy units, and on through the months of October and November, where it was not always by any means a walk over, and where the urgent necessity for pressing on the heels of the Boches afforded no time or opportunity for rest.
<small>CHARACTERISTICS.</small>

In the London Territorial can be found all the qualities that go to make the highest standard of assault troops : he is alert, courageous, enduring, intelligent, and ready to act on his own initiative. An enemy Intelligence Summary captured at Menin Lietard paid a high compliment to the 58th (London) Division as being " excellent storm troops." What the Londoner dislikes is boredom ; if he is bored—and that can only be the fault of his officers—he will soon deteriorate and become stale, flat, and unprofitable. The long weary vigils of trench warfare must be made interesting to him, and not be a mere routine of monotonous duties ; working parties, routine duties and training must be livened up ; his interest must be aroused in everything and at all times. Here is about the best fighting material in the British forces, if properly handled. The responsibility of those in command of such material is great, but it is well repaid if the material is tactfully and intelligently directed.
<small>GENERALLY.</small>

Belgium, 1919.

III

BATTLE HONOURS OF THE POST OFFICE RIFLES, AUGUST, 1914, TO NOVEMBER, 1918

Festubert	... May, 1915.
Loos	September, 1915.
Vimy	... May, 1916.
Somme—High Wood	September, 1916.
,, Butte de Warlencourt	October, 1916.
Bullecourt—Village	... May, 1917.
,, Hindenburg Line	June, 1917.
Ypres—Messines	June, 1917.
,, Wurst Farm	September, 1917.
,, Passchendaele	October, 1917.
Cambrai—Bourlon Wood	November, 1917.
St. Quentin—Crozat Canal	March, 1918.
,, Tergnier	March, 1918.
,, Noreuil	March, 1918.
,, Chauny	March, 1918.
Defence of Amiens—Villers Bretonneux	April, 1918.
Somme—Malard Wood	August, 1918.
,, Chipilly	August, 1918.
,, Billon Wood	August, 1918.
,, Marrieres Wood	August, 1918.
,, Epehy and Peizieres	September, 1918.
,, Ronnsoy	September, 1918.
Loos to Bauffe—Lens	October ⎫
,, Annay	⎪
,, Courrieres	to ⎬ 1918.
,, Wattines	⎪
,, The Scheldt	November ⎭

IV

THE POST OFFICE RIFLES,
1914 TO 1918

1. PRELIMINARY.

WHEN the official history of the Post Office Rifles comes to be written, much will no doubt be said about the difficulties, common to all units, of organization in the early days of the great war. England was not prepared for a war on a colossal scale, and the machinery for carrying it out had to be hastily improvised, much being left to the ingenuity and enthusiasm of individuals. Great credit is due, therefore, to those pre-war Territorial officers and men who came forward and gave their time, money, and experience to the organization of the Post Office Rifles in those troublous days. To their energy is due the early demand of the Battalion to be sent to a theatre of active hostilities, the magnificent response in recruits, and the facilities for the training and equipment of a unit which was fit for active service several months before it actually left for France.

ORGANIZATION.

By September, 1914, the Battalion was not only complete in every detail, but had a large reserve, which was itself formed into a separate unit and designated as 2/8th Battalion. Later a third line was formed, and known as the 3/8th or 8th (Reserve) Battalion. Thus, while the 8th or Post Office Rifles still remained an integral Battalion of the City of London Regiment, it also became a Regiment in itself, consisting of two fighting units, the 1/8th and 2/8th, and a Reserve Battalion, the 3/8th.

As much depends on the supply and efficiency of reinforcements, a few words about the Reserve Battalion would not be out of place. Originally drafts for the 1/8th in France were sent from the 2/8th, but since its formation in 1915, the Reserve Battalion has sent 222 officers and nearly 5,000 men to the Post Office Rifles in France. On one occasion—in September, 1918—it was sent, as a unit, to quell strike disturbances at Newport, but happily had a bloodless journey. It has also provided Guards of Honour to His Majesty the King, at Aldershot, July 24th, 1917 (officer in charge, Lieutenant H. C. Diss), at the Memorial Service, Westminster Abbey,

THE RESERVE BATTALION.

July 11th, 1918 (officer in charge, Captain T. P. Croysdale), and to His Royal Highness the Duke of Connaught, at Blackdown, October, 1918 (officer in charge, Captain E. B. Davies, M.C.).

The first Commanding Officer of the Reserve Battalion was Lieutenant-Colonel F. Owen, T.D., who was also responsible for the start of the 2/8th, and who for over two and a half years rendered untiring and most valuable service to the Regiment. In April, 1917, he was succeeded by Lieutenant-Colonel B. Davie. In January, 1918, Lieutenant-Colonel P. E. Langworthy Parry took over the command, and infused much energy into the tactical training of officers and men.

COMMITTEES. Before proceeding to the fighting story of the Regiment, mention must be made of the ungrudging support, both financial and otherwise, given by the Postal Authorities, and the really excellent work of the various committees formed to look after the comfort of the men. The thousands of pairs of socks, the scarves, mittens, candles, footballs, books, magazines, boxing-gloves, games, and, above all, cigarettes, provided by these committees have administered largely to the well-being and recreation of all ranks, and entailed no little labour and self-sacrifice on the part of the friends of the Regiment. These committees have now been centralized into " The Post Office Rifles Benevolent Institution," with an influential committee under the Presidency of Colonel Sir Andrew Ogilvie, K.B.E., C.B. Communications for help and advice should be addressed to the Secretary, Mrs. Percy Ash, 130, Bunhill Row, E.C. 1.

2. THE 1/8TH BATTALION.

EARLY DAYS. The Post Office Rifles, like many other Territorial units, were on the way to their annual Training Camp when the news of the impending great struggle was received. The Battalion returned to London, and on the declaration of war was embodied and billeted in the various Post Offices of the Metropolis. Three of the eight companies acquired comfortable quarters in King Edward's Building, of the General Post Office, empty mail-bags, precursors of the generally useful sand-bags, being found to make fair substitutes for beds. After rapid moves, much marching, and frequent changes of billets, which provided a useful experience of what was to come in France, the Battalion eventually pulled up at Crowborough, where training commenced in earnest. Here many changes took place: a large number of the Battalion were transferred to the R.E., Army Post Office

CROWBOROUGH.

and the Telegraph Section. In November, 1914, the
5th London (London Rifle Brigade) left the Brigade to go
to France, and the 6th, 7th, and 8th Battalions were
transferred to the 2nd London Division (afterwards
known as the 47th [London] Division), to take the place
of the 13th (Kensingtons), 14th (London Scottish), and
16th (Queen's Westminsters), which had been sent to
France. The 15th (Civil Service Rifles) formed the
4th Battalion of the 140th Brigade. At Abbots Langley, ABBOTS
where the Battalion had now moved, final preparations LANGLEY.
were made for foreign service. The four-company organization was introduced in January, 1915, and training
became strenuous. There were many alarms and ex-
cursions, including one in the early dawn of Boxing Day,
which will not easily be forgotten. The Battalion also
had the privilege of assisting in lining the streets on the
occasion of the funeral of that grand old warrior Lord
Roberts.

On St. Patrick's Day (March 17th), 1915, a start was FRANCE.
made for France (Havre). After a brief stay at the
camp on the hill, probably the bleakest and most uncomfortable spot in any theatre of war, the Battalion entrained
for Auchel, and moved thence to Bethune to get a first
experience of trench warfare. The principal personnel
of the Battalion on landing in France was—Lieutenant-
Colonel J. Harvey, in Command, Major E. Hood, Second-in-
Command, Captain T. Morris (Rifle Brigade), Adjutant,
Lieutenant Fairley, Quartermaster, and R.S.M. Witheridge,
on Headquarters; and "A" Company, Captain Milne and
C.S.M. Carty; "B" Company, Captain Davie and C.S.M.
Radley; "C" Company, Captain Gore Browne and C.S.M.
Dunkling; and "D" Company, Captain Maxwell and
C.S.M. Etheridge. Of these names, only one will be
found in connection with the Post Office Rifles in France
on Armistice Day, 1918—that of Brigadier-General Max-
well, C.M.G., D.S.O., commanding the Brigade in which
this Battalion was then included.

The 8th were fortunate in having the 4th Guards GIVENCHY.
Brigade (under Lord Cavan), of the 2nd Division, as their
tutors in trench warfare, and all ranks owe a deep debt
of gratitude to that Brigade, not only for the excellent
instruction, but for the courtesy and patience with which
it was imparted.

In the first spell of trenches, near Givenchy, two
officers were killed (Captain West and Lieutenant McCabe)
by an enemy shell smashing up a so-called dug-out at
French Farm. The Battalion remained in this vicinity
until May, and were in support at Annequin when the BATTLE OF
fighting commenced at Festubert. These operations, May, 1915.

which lasted from May 9th until near the end of the month, were designed to support the French attack some miles south at Souchez. On May 16th, while the attack was being continued in the neighbourhood, Richebourg, by the 2nd Division, the Battalion moved into the line at Festubert, and sustained many casualties. La Quinque, the Yellow Road, Willow Road, Welsh Chapel, and Dead Cow Farm, will bring back reminiscences of a not altogether pleasant nature to many who were there. On the 22nd "B" and "C" Companies took over portions of the old Hun line, which had been captured, and on the following day attacked and cleared some hundreds of yards of enemy territory, losing Lieutenants Hatfield and Moon (killed), and heavy casualties in other ranks. "C" Company having been heavily shelled, it was left to "D" Company to continue the attack, relying on bombs, with which, however, the enemy were better and more plentifully supplied. After obtaining the assistance of bombers of King Edward's Horse, the attack was successfully renewed on the 25th, and more enemy trenches taken, a strong point, known as J.3, holding out and defying capture. A further attack on this strong point was ordered for the morning of the 26th, but, fortunately, postponed to allow the position to be bombarded by heavy artillery. Some enemy who were seen to be retiring provided interesting and useful target practice.

When the Battalion eventually advanced to attack this post, an unforeseen incident occurred which materially assisted the attack. Some neighbouring British troops on the right moved in the direction of J.3, which they thought to be in British hands, at the very moment that the Post Office Rifles were commencing to attack it. This was too much for the Boche garrison, who hoisted the white flag and allowed the Post Office Rifles to capture one officer, forty other ranks, and some machine guns. So ended the first experience of the Battalion in actual battle, and gave them a reputation as a fighting unit which was well sustained in future contests. If the casualties were severe (in addition to those named, 2nd-Lieutenants Oliver Lawrence and Maclebone were killed, and 50 per cent. of other ranks killed and wounded), at any rate the enemy, whose artillery was many times stronger than the British, suffered quite as heavily, judging from the number of their dead lying around the captured territory, and also lost some tactical positions.

MAROC. After periods of rest at Philosophe and in the line by the Hulluch Road and Vermelles, the Battalion found themselves at Maroc, the Garden City, then a very agreeable place with good houses and gardens, and only slightly visited by " Hun hate." A period of training at La Bouverie, and a return visit to Maroc—not quite so pleasant a spot as on the previous tour there—filled up the interval until the September offensive against Loos.

BATTLE OF Loos, September, 1915.

The 140th Brigade were on the extreme right of the attacking forces. The primary attack was to be made by the 6th and 7th Battalions, with the 8th in close support. The approach march from Les Brebis to assembly positions, which normally would occupy two hours, owing to congestion of troops, took over five hours.

Gas was to be used for the first time by the British. Great secrecy had been observed as to its probable use, and great things were expected from it. The wind, however, did not play the game, and the gas, which was ejected from cylinders, was not a success. Smoke, gas, and uncut wire proved considerable obstacles in keeping good direction, and as a result there was soon a big gap between the 6th and 7th Battalions. The main rôle of the 8th was to support the pivot of the attack, the famous Double Crassier, and their assistance was soon required. The enemy made a determined counter-attack from south of the Crassier, and, fighting gallantly against superior numbers, the 7th were driven back. A bombing platoon of the 8th, under Lieutenant Thomas, was at once ordered over, and pressed the enemy back in fine style. They were reinforced by " A " and " B " Companies of the 8th, " C " and " D " Companies following later. The Double Crassier was a source of continual trouble with nightly bombing encounters, until the Battalion was relieved on September 30th. The Battalion had every reason to be proud of their part in this battle. They came in at a critical and nasty moment, and succeeded in re-establishing the success achieved by others in the first instance. Fortunately, the casualties were comparatively light.

After a short rest the Battalion went into the line near Lone Tree, to support an attack by the 1st Division at Hulluch. This attack was not a success, and the Battalion took over the front line from three attenuated Battalions of the 1st Division, who had suffered severely from trench mortars. Consequently the line was held very lightly, and few casualties occurred. One unlucky trench mortar, however, demolished a party of six who, in spite of orders against congregating together, were seated at breakfast in a dangerous spot.

LONE TREE, October 13th, 1915.

About this time Lieutenant-Colonel Harvey, who had steered the Battalion through its initiation into active warfare, went home sick, and Lieutenant-Colonel A. Maxwell assumed command. Captain Morris, the Adjutant, also left to command a Service Battalion of the Rifle Brigade. His work with the Battalion should not pass unnoticed. Much of the efficiency of the Post Office Rifles is due to his untiring efforts and to his willing help and assistance in every direction. He was succeeded by Captain Hume-Peel, who had been acting as Assistant Adjutant.

BOIS HUGO. An uncomfortable spell at Bois Hugo, north of Loos, followed. Continuous wet weather had turned the trenches into drains, with an average depth of two feet of water everywhere, which defied all efforts to remedy by pumping. Enemy 5·9's enfiladed most portions of the front line system, and the loose nature of the soil prevented any effective repair. The trenches were either blown in by continuous shelling or spontaneously collapsed in the most disheartening manner. Casualties were appreciable, and there were some cases of trench feet, the first which had occurred in the Battalion. The line was thinned out as much as was compatible with safety. After a short tour of duty by the Chalk Pit Sector, the Division was relieved, and the Battalion LILLERS. moved to Lillers in November, where the change to houses, shops, and a canteen was greatly appreciated. Expeditionary Force canteens had only just been started in front areas, and were very primitive affairs compared to those of later times.

HOHENZOLLERN. Shortly before Christmas the Battalion moved into the Hohenzollern Sector, which was by no means a health resort. This stay proved to be short, and the Battalion managed to avoid the Hun efforts to blow them up with mines. Another visit to Maroc, to relieve the French, provided an interesting incident in the general "wind up" on the occasion of the Kaiser's birthday, which, however, passed off peacefully enough. A couple of LOOS. tours in a sector adjoining Loos were sufficiently exciting, as the Battalion was sitting—quite comfortably, as it turned out—over a Hun mine which was "certain to go up in twenty-four hours." Bombing encounters took place nightly. At first honours were easy in this respect, but the 8th bombers gradually drew away and established a superiority, finally giving the enemy a severe and decided trouncing.

SOUCHEZ, After a short rest at Lillers, the Battalion was trans-
March, 1916. ferred to a new district. *En route*, a week's stay was made at Gouy Servins, where much sanitary work had to be done, and where the Battalion celebrated the anniversary of its landing in France. The Souchez district will bring back varied memories—of the Zouave Valley, or "Valley of Death," as it was commonly called ; the

Pimple, a horrid excrescence in the Boche lines, all eyes
and guns; the Lorette Spur, a hive of O.P.'s from where
one could see far into " Germany," and the happy hunt-
ing-ground of F.Os., Staff Officers, Corps Observers, and
Cook's tourists; Souchez, a mere collection of broken
bricks, timber, and small ditches; Ablain, Carency,
Villers-au-Bois, Verdrel, and Estree Cauchee; appalling
front-line trenches, either water-courses or barricades
built of mining débris; " Minnies " of all calibres, chiefly
heavy, destroying in a minute the arduous labour of many
nights; and, most wonderful of all, the almost disused
rear communication trenches, overhung with poppies
and cornflowers, which gave a riot of gorgeous colour
to the otherwise bare wastes of war.

Little by little the defences of the Souchez Sector
had been made tolerable, when the Division side-slipped
to the south, and took over in addition the Carency and
Berthonval Sectors. Immediately prior to this mines
had been blown up, and an attack, partially successful,
made to secure a certain crater area. Reconnoitring
parties of the 8th were not favourably impressed with
the new positions, and after running into a Boche " strafe "
of no small extent, with difficulty escaped from an enemy
counter-attack on the craters, where several prisoners
were taken. When the Battalion arrived on the following
night (May 19th) it was found that the Boches had been
continually throwing heavy " Minnies " on to the front
line, and had also succeeded in demolishing Battalion
Headquarters; the crater line was wrecked and exposed
on both flanks, the front line proper practically obliterated,
and the communication trenches blown in in many places.
On Saturday (20th) the Boches renewed their " Minnie "
strafe with disastrous results on the remaining pieces of BATTLE OF VIMY RIDGE, May 21st, 1916.
trench. The whole Battalion, assisted by large working
parties, were employed on building up the line, and urgent
calls were made for artillery retaliation. The " Minnies "
continued their deadly work on Sunday morning, but
finished about midday, and all ranks looked forward to
a quiet afternoon in preparation for a busy night. About
3 p.m. the quiet was disturbed by the fire of 100 enemy
batteries concentrated on a front of 2,500 yards. The
section held by the Battalion became a lurid inferno.
There was nothing to be done, however, but to stick it
out and await developments. At 8 p.m., after five hours
of the most intense bombardment ever experienced in
France either before or since this date, the Huns blew
up more mines and attacked in force. The enemy soon
overran the crater line, captured the few who remained
in the front line, and secured the two first British lines
on Vimy Ridge. The Battalion bombers, led by

Lieutenant King and "C" Company, made an immediate counter-attack, which succeeded in pinning the enemy down in the captured lines. The arrival of two companies of the 15th London made it possible to arrange another counter-attack on a larger scale, though all the Lewis guns of the 8th and of the companies of the 15th had been destroyed. The counter-attack was made by the two companies of the 15th, a weak company of the 18th, the survivors of the 8th and 7th, and two companies of the 6th Battalion, and, reaching the Hun line on the left, succeeded in arresting any further advance of the enemy. Relief came on the Monday. The Battalion had done extraordinarily well under the most adverse conditions. The attack by the Boches, which had been carefully prepared with large numbers of batteries massed to cover a confined space, was evidently intended to delay the impending British offensive on the Somme, and to secure Vimy Ridge, Zouave Valley, and the Cabaret Rouge Ridge, and so threaten the flanks of the British lines in that region. That the enemy failed was due to the tenacity and grit of the 47th Division, which refused to admit of defeat.

VIMY COUNTER-ATTACK, May 22nd, 1916.

Casualties were severe: "A," "B," and "D" Companies were practically wiped out, the C.O. (Lieutenant-Colonel A. Maxwell) severely wounded, and many other officers and men killed or wounded.

CAMBLAIN CHATELAIN, May-June, 1916.

On the night of May 22nd-23rd the Brigade was relieved, and the Battalion proceeded via Camblain l'Abbé to billets at Camblain Chatelain (commonly called "Charlie Chaplin"), where they remained for three weeks, during which time drafts were received and the Battalion reorganized. Lieutenant-Colonel Whitehead was now in command.

SOUCHEZ, June, 1916.

About the end of June the Battalion returned to the Souchez Sector, still famous for the depth of water to be found in the trenches. Appropriately the Hawke Battalion of the Royal Naval Division (lately returned from Gallipoli) was attached for instructional duties, and were soon at home in their natural element. A move was soon made back to the Vimy Sector, and the same section of the line as had been the scene of the battle on May 21st.

CAOURS, July-August, 1916.

On July 21st a long trek began to the Abbeville area for training, in anticipation of further fighting on the Somme. The weather was intensely hot for marching with full equipment. Short stays were made *en route* at the villages of Estree Cauchee (obviously and always called "Extra Cushy"), Ourton, Brias, Blangerval, Villers Hospital, and Conteville, until Caours was reached, where the Battalion had two weeks' hard training. From here the Battalion marched to Franvillers, staging at

Vauchelles, Naours, and Beaucourt. At Round Wood, FRANVILLERS. near Franvillers, the training for the attack was completed on a taped trench system, and the Battalion was ready to take part in the projected attack on High Wood. This BATTLE OF HIGH wood had already been the scene of many sanguinary WOOD, September 14th, 1916. fights, but, being an important tactical position, its possession had always been hotly contested by the Boches, in whose hands it still remained. The rôle of the Battalion was partly to pass through the 15th Battalion, who had to make the first assault on the wood, and partly to take the 2nd and 3rd enemy lines to the right of the wood.

On September 13th the Battalion moved to Becourt Wood, and on the following night to assembly lines in the wood. This was the first occasion in which tanks were used, and though they did great work in the neighbouring village of Flers, they were unable to get through the wood. On the right the enemy second and third lines were carried, and High Wood was finally cleared of the enemy about noon with the help of the 140th Trench Mortar Battery, who fired 700 rounds into the wood in twenty minutes.

On the 18th a highly successful attack was made on BATTLE OF the Flers line, after which the Battalion was relieved FLERS, September 18th, 1916. and moved to Henencourt.

Casualties in these operations were heavy—eight officers killed (Captains Mitchell, Webb, and Chichester, and 2nd-Lieutenants Potter, Coote, Kennedy, Burrows, and Matthews) and four officers wounded (2nd-Lieutenants Diss, Raphael, Willows, and Trenchard); 2nd-Lieutenant Cook was missing, and of other ranks there were about 300 killed and wounded.

After being reinforced and reorganized, the Battalion BATTLE OF was moved up via Eaucourt l'Abbé, and on the following BUTTE DE WARLENCOURT, October 7th, 1916. day made a somewhat disastrous attack on the famous Butte de Warlencourt, a mound which bristled with unsuspected machine guns. Two companies were completely wiped out, only seven men returning. The casualties in this attack were three officers killed (Lieutenant Snowden, 2nd-Lieutenants Stirling and Jenkins) and seven wounded (2nd-Lieutenants Kirby, Smith, Starling, Watson, Macbeth, and Everson, and Captain Thomas), while 2nd-Lieutenant Leon was missing. Casualties to other ranks numbered 400.

On October 9th the remnants of the Battalion were moved to Albert, and entrained on the 13th for the Ypres YPRES SALIENT, Salient, where the Battalion was to remain for eleven October, 1916. uncomfortable months, relieved by some historic fighting. to June, 1917,

D

The severe fighting on the Somme and the heavy casualties incurred there necessitated a reorganization of the Battalion. Officers were attached from other Battalions both to command companies and platoons, and considerable reinforcements were required to bring the Battalion up to effective strength.

The sector allotted to the 47th Division extended from the northern bank of the Ypres-Commines Canal (more familiarly known as the Bluff) to about 300 yards north of Hill 60, and in the course of several months the Battalion became well acquainted with every portion of the sector. In May, 1917, the Division relinquished the Northern Brigade front, and took over a Brigade section of the 41st Division south of the canal. It was from the latter section that the Battalion attacked on June 7th, 1917.

The Ypres Salient was never a " cushy " place, and the part held by the 47th Division could hardly be said to afford a rest-cure to the troops holding it. The ground was water-logged ; " trenches " consisted mostly of sand-bagged barricades built above the level of the ground, while shell-proof dug-outs were conspicuous by their absence. Trench mortars of all calibres were particularly playful on both sides, and the artillery, in which the superiority of the British was very marked, conspired to make day and night hideous, and to render the naturally uncomfortable conditions about as unpleasant as it is possible to imagine. Raids were frequent, especially on the side of the enemy, who seemed suspicious of an impending attack, and were consequently jumpy and anxious to secure information.

During this period of trench warfare many changes took place in the Battalion. Lieutenant-Colonel Whitehead went to England sick in November, 1916, and for some months the Battalion was commanded by senior Captains, until Major Vince assumed command, with Major Balfour, of the Northern Cyclists' Battalion, as Second-in-Command. Captain Peel, who had been Adjutant for a considerable time, was attached to Brigade Headquarters, and his duties were taken over by 2nd-Lieutenant Jacob. In March, 1917, Lieutenant-Colonel Vince went to England on a course at the Senior Officers' School, Aldershot ; and Lieutenant-Colonel Maxwell, who had sufficiently recovered from his wounds to return to France, took over the command of the Battalion. Major Balfour was transferred to the 1/15th Battalion, his place being taken by Captain R. S. Johnson, also of the Northern Cyclist Battalion.

About the beginning of May, 1917, the whole of the 140th Brigade were withdrawn to a training area near St. Omer to rehearse the projected attack on the Messines Ridge. Brigadier-General Viscount Hampden, who had commanded the Brigade since June, 1916, went to England sick, and was replaced by Brigadier-General Kennedy, who had previously commanded the 21st Battalion in the same Division.

BATTLE OF MESSINES, June 3rd to 12th, 1917.

The Battalion was billeted at Quercamp during the training period; their portion of the attack was very thoroughly rehearsed on a dummy trench system constructed to represent the enemy trenches. In the last week of May the Battalion returned to the forward area, and moved into the line on the night of June 3rd-4th for the grand attack timed for 3.10 a.m. on June 7th. The journey to the line was distinctly unpleasant. All usual routes were assiduously deluged with H.E. and gas, but by selecting a somewhat devious route the Battalion, in spite of several warm moments, arrived with practically no casualties.

The plan of attack, so far as the infantry were concerned, was as follows :—

The 47th Division was to attack astride the Ypres-Commines Canal with two Brigades—the 140th Brigade south, and the 142nd Brigade north of the Canal—the 141st Brigade being in support. Each attacking Brigade had two Battalions in front to attack and consolidate the first four lines of enemy trenches, including certain strong points and enemy positions on the Canal banks. Three hours after zero the remaining Battalions of the attacking Brigade were to pass through and capture further enemy positions to a total depth of about 1,000 yards.

The 1/8th Battalion, under command of Lieutenant-Colonel A. Maxwell, were included in the first phase of the attack, and formed the right flank of the 47th Division. On their right was the 11th Queen's (41st Division), and on their left the 1/7th Battalion London Regiment. Their objectives comprised portions of the four lines known as Oak Trench, Oak Support, Oak Reserve, and Oak Switch, and included, in addition to a number of communication trenches, a formidable strong point constructed at the northern end of a road known as the Dammstrasse.

During the three days immediately preceding the attack the bombardment of our artillery was intense, and, as ascertained later, exceptionally deadly. So much was the morale of the enemy affected that our men could look over the top in broad daylight without the smallest danger, except from fragments from our own shells ; most platoon commanders were able to take their men to their jumping-off positions, and show them objects in the Hun lines to guide their advance. On the night of June 6th-7th the Battalion was assembled waiting for the anxious moment of zero. Gradually the bombardment died down, until at 3.10 a.m. on the 7th, along the battle front of ten miles, nineteen large mines were exploded as the signal for attack. Some of these mines had been under construction for more than two years ; those nearest the Battalion were at St. Eloi on the right and Hill 60 on the left. The effect of these huge explosions was terrific, and never likely to be forgotten by those who took part in this fight. If the first sensation was almost paralyzing to our own troops, the shock to the enemy was overwhelming. The barrage opened at the same moment, and the attack commenced, while the enemy batteries were being neutralized by torrents of gas shells. It is hardly a matter of surprise that under these conditions the enemy resistance was feeble in the earlier objectives, even the much-dreaded Dammstrasse being captured without serious opposition. Many of the casualties of the Battalion were due to machine-gun fir from the White Château, one of the objectives of the 7th Battalion. This was a naturally strong position, and so well fortified that a determined garrison might have held out for a long time. Some of the 1/8th took part in the attack on this Château, and materially assisted in its capture. Corporal Bottomley, of the 1/8th, made his way into the place through deadly machine-gun and rifle fire, and, capturing one of the machine guns which was doing most of the damage to our men, proceeded to use it on the enemy themselves. Unfortunately, he was not long to survive this heroic act, for when the place was finally taken his dead body was found across the very gun he had so gallantly captured and used. By this time the enemy was thoroughly demoralized, and no difficulty was encountered in capturing, consolidating, and holding all the objectives, although the enemy kept up a continuous bombardment on the whole of the sector, causing several casualties. So ended for this Battalion an historic fight, one remarkable for the extraordinarily careful organization and preparation of every detail. For the next five days the Battalion remained in the captured area until the Division was relieved, when they proceeded to Reninghelst, and then to Lynde to rest and refit.

From June 3rd to 12th the Battalion had lost two officers killed (Captain A. T. Davis and 2nd-Lieutenant

E. Henderson) and six officers wounded (Captain C. B. Fenwick, Lieutenant T. C. H. Berry, 2nd-Lieutenants Foster, Billham, Peters, and James). The casualties to other ranks were about 200, of whom about 40 were killed. Compared to the casualties on the Somme, these were extremely light.

After a fortnight's rest the Battalion returned to the forward area, when Lieutenant-Colonel De Vesian took command, Lieutenant-Colonel Maxwell leaving to command the 1/23rd Battalion (142nd Brigade), which command he retained until appointed to a Brigade command in June, 1918. Major Vince became Second-in-Command. For the next few weeks the Battalion was doing the usual tours of line duty, both in its old sector and in front of Hooge ; and later, after the unsuccessful attack on Polygon Wood on July 31st, they occupied a shell-hole line on the Westhoek Ridge, probably one of the most unpleasant resorts of Belgium or France ; here the enemy artillery, which had recovered from the June attack, became annoyingly active. In addition to tours of line duty, preparations were being made for the series of autumn attacks in the salient, such as laying waterpipes, making dumps, duck-board tracks, etc. On September 14th Lieutenant-Colonel De Vesian left to take up another appointment, and Major Vince again took up the command of the Battalion, with Captain Johnson as Second-in-Command. *YPRES SALIENT, July to September, 1917.*

On September 17th the Division was withdrawn to the Arras front, a welcome relief after eleven continuous months in the Ypres Salient. Since the Battle of Messines the Battalion had suffered many casualties, including two officers killed (2nd-Lieutenant Cooke and 2nd-Lieutenant Sanders) and several wounded, amongst others Captain A. Thomas, M.C., 2nd-Lieutenant W. B. Will, M.C., and Lieutenant H. A. Appleton. *ARRAS, September to November, 1917.*

On September 25th the Battalion moved into the line at Gavrelle, which had been the scene of heavy fighting in the spring of 1917. Things, however, were very quiet now, and the change was much appreciated. Nothing of particular interest occurred while holding the Gavrelle—Oppy sector ; even a raiding party, under 2nd-Lieutenant B. J. Fryer, which successfully entered the enemy trenches, were unable to find any enemy there. About the middle of October Major E. J. Woolley, M.C., of the 1/22nd Battalion, became Second-in-Command, *vice* Captain Johnson, sick.

In November the Division was ordered to Italy, and moved into a back area to refit. Circumstances, however, *BATTLE OF CAMBRAI, November, 1917.*

decreed a change of programme, owing to developments in the Battle of Cambrai, and the Division was placed at the disposal of General Byng, commanding the Third Army. The Division moved by rapid stages until, on November 28th, the 8th Battalion was occupying a portion of the Hindenburg support line east of the Canal du Nord and facing Graincourt, acting as supports to the 1/6th and 1/15th (the latter actually being in Bourlon Wood, with the 1/6th just outside the wood on their left).

On the morning of November 30th the enemy attacked in force on a front extending from Bourlon Wood to Moeuvres. This front was held by three Divisions only —the 47th, 2nd, and 59th—who successfully held up the attack of seven enemy Divisions. At noon on that day the 1/6th were heavily engaged, and the 1/8th were moved up to support them. A counter-attack which was launched by headquarter details of the 1/6th and " A " Company of the 1/8th checked the enemy advance, and enabled a new line to be established 300 yards in rear of the old line. During the next forty-eight hours there was much shifting about of units, owing to the withdrawal of the 1/6th and 1/15th, who had suffered severely. This Battalion had to dig in under fire from machine guns and snipers on four different occasions.

On the night of December 2nd-3rd two companies (" A " and " C ") of the 1/8th and two companies of the 1/7th made an attack, which resulted in the re-establishment of the original line and the capture of fifty-six prisoners and sixteen machine guns. The Battalion, which was relieved on the following night, had lost as a result of the Cambrai operations one officer killed (2nd-Lieutenant P. S. Bishop), one missing (2nd-Lieutenant Higgerty), and six wounded (2nd-Lieutenants McKenzie, Playfoot, Fryer, Hainsworth, Miles, and Scott), and of other ranks about 170.

Rest was short at this period, for on December 5th the Battalion was holding the Hindenburg support line just north of Flesquieres, when the Cambrai Salient was finally evacuated. Matters soon quieted down, and after four days' rest at Bertincourt the Battalion was in the line until December 20th, when it was withdrawn to Mericourt l'Abbé. Here the Battalion, for the first time since its arrival in France, was allowed to spend Christmas out of the line. The occasion was celebrated appropriately.

January, 1918. In the middle of January, after a tour in the line at Ribemont, orders came for the dispersal of the Battalion.

"A" and "B" Companies were sent to reinforce the 1/17th, and "C" Company to the 1/24th Battalions. "D" Company was split up amongst the other companies and headquarters. The nucleus left over was amalgamated with the 2/8th, which then became the 8th Battalion, in the 58th Division.

Military requirements, no doubt, prompted the dispersal of this unit and of other first- or second-line units, partly owing to the difficulty of their being reinforced, and partly owing to the necessity of other units being reinforced; still, for those officers and other ranks who had made the 1/8th their military home for so long, and had fought together so often and so successfully, it was a hard blow to find that they were to be scattered in many directions and that the 1/8th as a separate unit had ceased to exist.

3. THE 2/8TH BATTALION.

EARLY DAYS, 1914.

The formation of a second-line Battalion of the 8th London Regiment took place in September, 1914, the first C.O. being Lieutenant-Colonel (then Captain) Owen. The personnel of the Battalion was composed of those who had not then volunteered for foreign service, reinforced by recruits. Training was carried out in Regent's Park and Victoria Park. Shortly after formation Major P. J. Preece, T.D., joined from the 1/8th, and superintended training on Hampstead Heath.

In November, 1914, the Battalion moved to billets in Cuckfield, with Lieutenant-Colonel Labouchere as Commanding Officer, Major Preece as Second-in-Command, and Captain Hoare as Adjutant. Here training continued for six months. During this period the Battalion was called upon to find drafts for the 1/8th in France, and continued to do so until it moved to Sutton Veny in July, 1916. Before this date, however, preliminary moves were made to Norwich, in May, 1915, and in June to Ipswich.

At Ipswich the training of the Battalion as a real unit commenced, though it was not until a later date (the end of 1915) that the third line of the 8th was in a position to send out reinforcements, and relieve the second line from this burden to a certain extent. Lieutenant-Colonel P. J. Preece was now in command, with Major E. de Vesian Second-in-Command, and Lieutenant H. W. Priestley Adjutant.

The final move took place in July, 1916, to Sutton Veny, where finishing touches were put to the training, preparatory to the Battalion proceeding to France as a unit of the 174th Brigade, 58th (London) Division.

France, January 27th, 1917. Arras Sector, February, 1917, to April, 1917.

The early days of this Battalion in France were not without interest. After landing at Havre on January 27th and concentrating at Villers l'Hospital, the Battalion proceeded to the Arras Sector, and served their instructional training in the line at Fonquevillers and Hannescamp.

After a short spell in the line at Bellacourt and rest billets at Bailleulmont, the Battalion relieved the 2/7th at Monchy au Bois, and found by reconnoitring patrols that the enemy was retiring. "C" Company, under Captain Ash, promptly worked its way across No Man's Land and occupied Ransart, establishing an outpost line there.

Bullecourt, April to June, 1917.

In April the Division was withdrawn to Bihucourt, and spent nearly a month (under canvas), working under R.E. direction, on the Ecoust-Mory Road in the neighbourhood of Bullecourt. This was by no means a pleasant job; there had been very severe fighting around Bullecourt in April and the beginning of May, in which the Australians had taken a conspicuous part, and all communications were plastered continuously with Boche metal.

In Bullecourt itself the situation was extraordinary. Parts of the village were in the enemy's hands, and parts occupied by British troops. The outpost positions changed almost hourly, and when the Battalion was sent up to relieve the remnants of H.A.C., Royal Welsh Fusiliers, and two Battalions of the Manchester Regiment, *Battle of Bullecourt Village.* the situation was, to say the best of it, obscure. Here the Battalion had its first taste of real fighting, for within forty-eight hours of taking up this line it was ordered to make a concerted attack with the 2/5th (L.R.B.) and clear the village of enemy. This was successfully accomplished, and a line established on the enemy's side of the village. By this time Bullecourt and its surroundings had become a veritable charnel-house; dead bodies and dead mules were lying about in hundreds, and the place was so offensive that it was a question whether it could be retained. Parties were organized to clear up, and in a short space of time, in spite of every adverse condition, it was made tolerably healthy. An amusing incident occurred in connection with five dead mules, which had become peculiarly offensive and defied all approach. The 2/8th undertook to remove the obstruction, and were given *carte blanche* as to methods. A party of twenty volunteers ("B" Company) were chosen under an officer; their report, which was forwarded to Brigade, is as follows:—

"The five dead mules are no longer offensive. The site of their grave is marked by an empty rum-jar, the contents of which materially assisted in the operation."

Changes took place in the Battalion. In May Lieutenant-Colonel P. J. Preece left to take up an appointment in England, and Lieutenant-Colonel A. D. Derviche-Jones (King's Own Royal Lancaster Regiment) took over the command; while Major de Vesian, who had become a Lieutenant-Colonel in the meantime, left to command the 1/8th.

The Battalion moved to the North Bullecourt Sector, and took part in an attack made by the 173rd Brigade (Brigadier-General Freyburg, V.C., D.S.O.) on the Hindenburg Line; two companies (" B " and " C ") were lent to the 2/1st Battalion (under the command of Lieutenant-Colonel Beresford), and attacked from Tiger Trench; and " D " Company (Captain Barnes) co-operated on the immediate north of Bullecourt. *BATTLE OF BULLECOURT— HINDENBURG LINE, June 16th, 1917.*

The attack, which lasted two days, was partially successful, in securing the first, but not the second, Hindenburg Line, but substantially improved the tactical position there.

Later the Battalion volunteered to get in a number of wounded of the 173rd Brigade who had been lying out in No Man's Land for several days. Other attempts to recover these men had failed. Forty-eight volunteers of " D " Company were selected, and were specially organized and trained during the day for this task. Led by 2nd-Lieutenant Richardson and the Padre (Vernon-Smith), every wounded man was got in, in spite of enemy opposition, and luckily without casualties.

In July, 1917, the Division moved to the Havrincourt Sector, then a delightful spot, where all kinds of fruits and vegetables could be picked during the intervals of enemy artillery strafes. The outpost lines were over 1,000 yards apart, and afforded much scope for skilful patrols. One patrol, under 2nd-Lieutenant Richardson, cleverly ambushed a Boche patrol, and accounted for the whole of them. A month's tour in this sector was exceedingly pleasant after Bullecourt, and passed without particular incident. At the end of July the Division moved to a training area behind Arras to prepare for the autumn offensives in the Ypres Salient. The Battalion was comfortably housed at Simencourt. Here Lieutenant-Colonel (then Major) C. B. Benson joined the Battalion as Second-in-Command; Captain Priestley, the Adjutant, left for England sick, and his duties were taken over by Captain T. J. Mumford. Training was fairly strenuous. Incidentally the Brigade organized a Sports and Assault-at-Arms Competition, which was won by this Battalion *HAVRINCOURT SECTOR, July, 1917.* *SIMENCOURT, August, 1917.*

with a first or second in each of the fifteen events. The Silver Cup, suitably inscribed, now forms part of the regimental plate.

YPRES, September, 1917, to January, 1918.

Towards the end of August the Division proceeded to Belgium, and on September 3rd this Battalion was in a shell-hole outpost line in the Alberta Sector just north of St. Julien. The enemy was exceedingly active with heavy artillery and gas shells. In the first four days' tour of this line the casualties exceeded 100. On September 9th a fairly successful raid was carried out by " D " Company under 2nd-Lieutenant Watson, who was unfortunately killed. From September 10th to 18th intensive training on a prepared ground was carried out, and on the night of the 19th-20th the Battalion assembled on a taped line for the attack on the Wurst Farm Ridge.

BATTLE OF WURST FARM RIDGE, September 20th, 1917.

The possession of this Ridge was essential to any successful attack on Passchendaele to the east; previous frontal attacks had failed with heavy casualties. A new plan of campaign was accordingly adopted; this ridge, which ran almost parallel to our line, north and south, culminating on the south at Wurst Farm, was to be attacked on a small frontage, some 800 yards' front on the north by one Battalion; another Battalion was then to pass through and wheel to the right, and yet a third to pass through again, wheel to the right, and capture Wurst Farm, thus securing in the first place access to the ridge on a small front, while others, by wheeling to the south, would cut off the enemy holding the rest of the ridge. In the meantime another Battalion would " mop up " the enemy who had been cut off. This method was entirely successful. A Boche officer taken prisoner said it was not fair, as a frontal fight all along the line had been expected by them and prepared for. The 51st (Highland) Division were to make an equally important attack on the left, and the 55th to co-operate on the right.

To the 2/8th was assigned the important honour of making the first breach to a depth of 1,000 yards, and securing the northern part of the ridge. The fighting strength of the Battalion (less nucleus) had been reduced to 430 rifles, and with this strength on an 800-yards' front a general frontal attack was doomed to failure. Normal formations were thrown to the wind, and, with the exception of a widely extended line of skirmishers, the attack was directed to secure the three main tactical positions of the enemy on this front—namely, the Marine View and concrete mebuses there; Genoa Farm, in the centre;

and Hubner Farm, an extremely strongly fortified and concreted farm, towards the left. The intervening spaces were practically neglected on the basis that if the three main tactical positions were taken the remainder of the line would fall. The difficulties were increased by the appalling state of the ground ; to get up to the assembly positions there was a single duck-board track, the position of which was well known to the enemy, who treated it with constant doses of every kind of poison. Across the Steenbeek, which had once been a stream, but was now, owing to incessant shelling, a wide morass of wet shell-holes, was a single duck-board bridge ; a party of men was constantly kept in a concrete mebus by the bridge to repair the bridge whenever and as soon as destroyed. Beyond the duck-board track in No Man's Land. was a piece of ground, every inch of which had been ploughed up by shells, and with the ever-present danger of finding oneself irretrievably bogged. No shelter was available except in old Boche concrete mebuses or farms, all of which were the target of a succession of 5'9's. To " A " Company was assigned Marine View and the mebuses there ; " C " Company the rest of the Promenade and Genoa Farm ; " B " Company a collection of ten mebuses, and with a roaming programme to assist " C " and " D " Companies ; and " D " Company, Hubner Farm. Battalion Headquarters were in Hibou Farm, a disgusting concrete shelter with the floor consisting of corrugated iron sheets supported on cross timbers, and with water (including two dead Boches) underneath. The assembly, which had been most carefully rehearsed, was accomplished with only one casualty ; and the men, who were in excellent spirits and full of confidence, were " out and over " the moment the barrage started, keeping in some instances within 10 yards of the barrage, and with our own shells bursting behind their backs. To recount all the details of the fight would take too long. It is sufficient to say that, in spite of the most strenuous opposition, and by dint of skilful manœuvres by Company Commanders and the utmost determination of all ranks, all objectives were taken. On the right and left the greatest difficulties were encountered, and all the officers of " A " and " C " Companies became casualties. Many deeds of heroism were performed : 2nd-Lieutenant Chancellor, shot through the lungs, stuck to his men until the last objective was taken, and then, when put on a stretcher, crawled off, saying that he would be damned if he would leave his men, and remained with them. 2nd-Lieutenant Richardson (then O.C. " C " Company), wounded in seven places, and 2nd-Lieutenant Mortimer, shot through the knees, struggled on with their men until all objectives had been taken and consolidated; and Sergeant Knight, whose heroic exploits gained the first V.C. for the Post Office Rifles. Hubner Farm was captured by the skilful command of Captain C. Kelly, of "D" Company, who, making use of some men of the 2/5th and some of the 9th Royal Scots to reinforce his sadly depleted Company, after a severe and protracted engagement, finally captured this farm with only thirteen men, taking over 100 unwounded and 30 wounded prisoners (including two Boche Medical Officers), and leaving a large number of enemy dead in the vicinity. Altogether some 250 unwounded prisoners, including four officers, were captured, together with a large number of machine guns. Great use was made of the bayonet, in which the men had been practised assiduously; and after the battle the famous 51st Division sent a high testimonial to the Battalion in saying that they fought like " bloody savages."

If the fighting was severe, the rewards were great—

1 V.C.;

1 D.S.O.;

8 Military Crosses (including 1 Bar);

2 D.C.Ms.; and

28 Military Medals.

After the breach made by this Battalion, the rest of the ridge was easily taken, with many prisoners, and five enemy counter-attacks were held off.

Casualties were heavy—three officers killed (2nd-Lieutenants Sloan, Blande, and Taylor) and six wounded (2nd - Lieutenants Chancellor, Richardson, Mortimer, Robinson, Hitch, and Edmonds); other ranks, 100 killed and 138 wounded.

LANDRETHUN, September-October, 1917. After being relieved, the Battalion went to a back area for rest and training. Pleasantly situated in wooded, undulating country at Landrethun, the Battalion had a good time. A Battalion Sports and Assault-at-Arms was won by " B " Company. Major Benson had been given the command of the 2/6th, and Major Barnes took his place as Second-in-Command.

POELCAPELLE, October, 1917, to January, 1918 About October 24th the Battalion came back to the line (in reserve) just north of where they had fought on September 20th. In the interval Poelcapelle had been captured, and the present line stretched from near Nobles' Farm, through Poelcapelle, Meunier and Tracas, south to the Lekkerbotterbeek.

On October 28th a sudden order was given to the Battalion to attack, in co-operation with one company of the 2/6th, on the night of October 29th-30th, in order to support the main attack by the Canadians on Passchendaele Ridge. On this occasion the state of the ground was even worse than on September 20th; there had been heavy rains in the meantime, and the duck-board tracks were some hundreds of yards short of the outpost line. The ground was almost unknown, and there was practically no time for reconnaissances. The men were guided on to the assembly line by carefully screened coloured lamps placed to show the boundaries of each company's front.

BATTLE OF PASSCHENDAELE, October 30th, 1917.

The objectives were Moray House, Papa Farm, Hinton Farm, and Cameron Houses, strong points lying between Poelcapelle and Passchendaele. From aeroplane photos the ground to be traversed seemed like a vast morass of mud and slime, as indeed it turned out to be. But little progress could be made. Men sank to their armpits in mud, and provided easy targets for the enemy. No support was forthcoming on the right. In spite of that, progress was made in the course of the day to about 500 yards, and outposts established, which, however, were ordered to be evacuated at night, except Nobles' Farm, which had been captured by the 2/6th on the left.

The casualties were very severe: five officers killed (Captains Wheeldon and Barnett, and 2nd-Lieutenants Duncan, McAllister, and Barnes) and five wounded (Lieutenant Shapley, and 2nd-Lieutenants Finch, Tinsley, Peacock, and Booth); and of other ranks, 34 killed, 173 missing (all believed to have been killed or drowned), and 42 wounded. To illustrate the state of the ground, four men tried for two hours with ropes to extricate a comrade, and failed. Though no objectives of this Battalion were taken, the main purpose of the attack was achieved, in that this lone Battalion, struggling against an even more implacable enemy than the Boches, drew so much artillery and machine-gun fire as to materially relieve the main attack on the Passchendaele Ridge.

About this time Major Soutten, of the 11th Battalion, joined as Second-in-Command.

After a rest spell at Escouilles ("Squeals"), the Battalion returned to the salient, and was mainly used for working parties at Poelcapelle.

ESCOUILLES.

The journey from Escouilles is worthy of remark. After staying the first day at Colomby, the Battalion started at 2 a.m., marched twelve kilometres to Wizernes, entrained for Elverdinghe, changed into a light railway for Kempton Park, marched and took up their position in support trenches at Pheasant Trench by 7 p.m. the same night.

Before leaving the 18th Corps at Ypres, the Corps Commander (Lieutenant-General Sir Ivor Maxse, K.C.B.) issued a farewell order to all the Divisions that had fought in his Corps. In this order he stated that, of the thirteen battles in which his Corps had taken part, the red-letter day was that of September 20th, 1917, and he especially praised the 51st (Highland) and the 58th (London) Divisions for their attacks on that day.

BARISIS, February and March, 1918. About January 6th, 1918, the whole Division was moved into the 3rd Corps, and, after detraining at Villers Bretonneux, the Battalion moved to Moreuil, and thence at the beginning of February to Pierremande, taking over from the 2nd Royal Scotch Fusiliers the southernmost portion of the British lines, at Barisis, with French troops on the right.

Barisis was a delightful spot, beautifully situated in the forest of Couchy, though it seemed likely to prove a storm-centre. The fact that an attack in force by the enemy was impending was well known to the authorities. The French told us that it would be from Barisis to the south, and the British were inclined to favour an attack from Barisis to the north. As it turned out, Barisis escaped the turmoil of battle, and the grand enemy attack started from some four miles to the north, at La Fere, extending from there to the north.

In the early days at Barisis the amalgamation with the 1/8th took place. There were now no longer two fighting lines of the 8th Battalion City of London Regiment.

4. THE 8TH BATTALION.

BARISIS. The first and primary job of the 174th Brigade was to put their sector into a respectable state of defence. With the exception of a tolerable front line, well wired, there was practically nothing to stop a break-through by the enemy. By arrangement, this Battalion, which had several French-speaking officers, was kept in the front line for long periods, and took on the job of deepening its defences. The 6th took on the battle zone, while the 7th provided working parties for all parts of the defence system.

Captain Mumford, who had been Adjutant of the 2/8th throughout the autumn fighting of the previous year, went home on substitute duty, and Captain Priestley became Adjutant of the 8th. The work was terrific, and admirably organized by the Brigade. By the date of the Boche attack formidable defences had been erected, well wired, well stocked, and well garrisoned. The importance of new defences for the Fifth Army front was well appreciated. The front was a very extended one (this Battalion held about 2,800 yards of front), and additional labour was scarce. Frequent visits were paid by all higher staffs, including General Gough, in command of the Fifth Army, who came twice to the Barisis Sector, and the Commander-in-Chief, Field-Marshal Sir Douglas Haig, who came personally with his Chief of Staff to see how the defences were progressing—a visit not without considerable danger to these distinguished personages from enemy "hate." Almost daily interviews took place with the French, and detailed arrangements were made for mutual support in the event of an attack. The relations between this Battalion and the French were most cordial; and if in the course of these three months they acquired an appreciation of canteen whisky, we certainly learned to relish their most excellent wines.

On the night of March 19th this Battalion was taken back to Pierremande to rest and provide working parties, and was the only Battalion of the Division in reserve when the grand enemy attack commenced at 4.30 a.m. on the morning of March 21st. BATTLE OF ST. QUENTIN, March 1918.

At 4.30 a.m. the Battalion was standing to arms, awaiting eventualities, but it was not until 5 p.m. that the order to move arrived, and the Battalion was embussed to Viry-Noreuil. In the ever-changing state of the battle it was difficult to get precise orders, and after reconnoitring various areas, it was only at 10.30 p.m. that the Battalion received definite orders to protect the crossings of the Crozat Canal from the Oise to about 3,000 yards north. The exact position of the enemy was unknown; it was possible that these crossings were already in the hands of the enemy. One map only was available for the Battalion, and no guides could be found. Moreover, the night was intensely foggy, though with a moon shining dimly through. A speedy move was urgent to prevent the enemy getting across the Oise and cutting off the 175th Brigade and the rest of the 174th Brigade holding from the Oise to Barisis. BATTLE OF CROZAT CANAL, March 21st-22nd.

At the last moment the G.O.C. 173rd Brigade (Brigadier-General Worgen), to which this Battalion was attached, arrived at Viry, having escaped from his Headquarters at Quessy, east of the canal, with the enemy only 200 yards away.

Plans were discussed and completed, and by midnight the Battalion was on its three-mile march to an unknown position in an unknown country—" C " and " D " Companies, under Captains Gunning and Kelly, on the right, and " A " and " B," under Captain Lanes and Lieutenant Lamb, on the left. The right companies found their way without difficulty, but the left companies were lost in the fog and open ground beyond the village of Tergnier, and it took the Battalion Headquarter Staff four hours to get them in position. Patrols on the enemy's side of the canal had failed to get in touch with the enemy when the morning of the 22nd dawned, though they had penetrated as far as Quessy, and removed important secret papers from Battalion Headquarters. All bridges were blown up by 4.30 a.m., patrols crossing on ruins of bridges or lock gates to rejoin their units. Owing to the fog, visibility was limited to an extreme of forty yards. Throughout the morning stragglers of the 173rd Brigade, who had been lost in the fog, came through our lines. About midday the enemy adopted the ruse of clothing parties of their men in the uniforms of captured or killed men of the 173rd Brigade, and by this means were enabled to put about a hundred men across at various places on our flank before they recommenced their attack at 1.15 p.m. Covered by an intense machine-gun barrage on the canal banks, and a bombardment of Battalion Headquarters in the Butte at Vouel, the enemy made a determined endeavour to secure the crossings in this Battalion's sector. On the right they failed, the crossings there being held for thirty-six hours by the remnants of " C " and " D " Companies, who eventually cut their way out after being surrounded on three sides. On the left the attack succeeded, mainly owing to the presence of the Boches dressed in British uniforms, who simultaneously attacked on the left and rear flank of the garrison. Very few of these two companies escaped, both Company Commanders being killed. From Battalion Headquarters at 4.30 p.m. streams of Boches, estimated at three to four battalions, could be seen pouring over the high ground west of the canal, and considerable execution was done amongst them with field artillery and massed machine guns. A line of defence was hastily manned, running from the Oise west of Tergnier, and further enemy attacks were arrested that day. By this time all lines of defence, except the canal crossings on

BATTLE OF TERGNIER, March 22nd-23rd.

the right, were being held by miscellaneous details; and after the Butte line had fallen, owing to an outflanking movement some two miles to the north, this Battalion was represented only by its Headquarter troops (strength about sixty) in the defence of Noreuil, and, on the 24th, of Chauny. On the right the remnants of "C" and "D" Companies held out to the afternoon of the 23rd, and then escaped to Condren, taking part in the defence of that place. At Chauny (night of 23rd-24th) the men were supplied with food and ammunition, both sorely needed. They had been living since the 21st merely on iron rations, while few had as many as five rounds of ammunition left, which were jealously guarded for desperate emergencies. The men were weary, too, from the continuous strain of marching, fighting, and digging in, and at Chauny were too worn out to dig defences, instead relying on ditches and natural folds in the ground. Later, after Chauny had fallen on the 25th, the remnants fell back on Besme, where they were reorganized, and sent to hold the crossings of the Oise at Quierzy for three more days. *BATTLE OF NOREUIL, March 23rd. BATTLE OF CHAUNY, March 24th. QUIERZY, March 25th.*

In the meantime the nucleus, which had been left at Pierremande with the 174th Brigade, were in trenches, covering the withdrawal of transport and stores. French reinforcements came up on the 23rd, but were ineffective in strange country and fog, and the burden of the defence was almost entirely borne by the worn-out British troops, assisted by Schools of Instruction and any able-bodied man who could be scraped up.

The casualties from March 21st had been heavy, and included thirteen officers, of whom four were killed (Captain Lanes, M.C., Lieutenant Lamb, and 2nd-Lieutenants Joyce and Edge), two wounded (Captains Gunning, M.C., and C. Kelly, M.C.), and seven wounded and missing (2nd-Lieutenants Odlafson, Wilkinson, Miller, Opet, Wheeler, Barnes, and Hewett). Of other ranks, more than 300 were killed, wounded, or missing. Splendid work had been done by the Battalion, especially by the right companies ("C" and "D," under Captains Gunning and Kelly) and by Headquarter details, amongst whom Major Soutten, M.C., Captain Priestley, 2nd-Lieutenant Ward, and the Medical Officer, Captain Massy-Miles, were conspicuous.

Major Soutten was now in command, when on March 29th a trek was made to St. Paul-aux-Bois, where the Battalion was employed day and night on working parties. On April 2nd and following days further treks were made to Audignicourt, and through the Valley of *DEFENCE OF AMIENS, April, 1918.*

VILLERS BRE-TONNEUX, April, 1918.
the Aisne to Dommier, thence to Longpoint, where the Battalion entrained, arriving the same night at Abbé Wood. Here reserve positions were taken up, until on April 13th the Battalion was moved up to the front line at Villers Bretonneux, where a draft of two companies of the 8th Norfolk Regiment, seven officers and 250 men, reinforced the Battalion, and Major Browne became Second-in-Command.

Villers Bretonneux will long live in the memory of those who had the misfortune to be there as one of the most unpleasant and hotly-contested positions in the defence of Amiens. Under continuous bombardment by day and night, by shells of all calibres—mostly gas—no place, not even the deepest cellar, afforded security. One gas shell knocked out ninety men of Headquarters' details, of whom fifty died from gas poisoning. From April 17th to 19th there were more than 150 gas casualties, including Lieutenant-Colonel Soutten, Major Browne, 2nd-Lieutenants Howes, Bruggemeyer, Ward, and Hawley; while Captain Massey-Miles, M.C., one of the whitest and most gallant Battalion Medical Officers in France, died of gas-poisoning after an heroic attempt to succour others similarly poisoned, removing his gas-mask in order to do so, and thus courting an inevitable and agonizing death. Three Medical Officers were sent in quick succession in one day, two of whom became casualties, one killed and one wounded. The last to arrive, Lieutenant Macbean, of the American Army, survived the ordeal, and remained with the Battalion until the end of the war.

DOMART. Lieutenant-Colonel Johnston took over the command on the 20th, with Major Edwards as Second-in-Command. Matters were still critical, and after a few days at Boutillerie the Battalion took up positions at Domart, until relieved by the French on the 27th, when they entrained to Neuf Moulin. In the last three days (25th-27th) one officer (2nd-Lieutenant Carter) was killed and two wounded (Captain Faber and Lieutenant Brown); while of other ranks 13 were killed, 83 wounded, and 43 gassed. The defence of Amiens was now secured, but at what cost! This story, bare of detail, of one Battalion during the terrible days of March and April, 1918, may read grimly enough, but this Battalion was one of many, and by no means exceptionally situated.

WARLOY, ALBERT. After a week at Neuf Moulin, the Battalion moved to Warloy, and was employed in digging defence lines. The Division subsequently relieved the 47th Division, the Battalion moving first into the Henencourt and then the

Albert Sectors, immediately in front of that town. About this time Lieutenant Jacob became Adjutant, *vice* Major Priestley, Second-in-Command.

On June 28th Brigadier-General A. Maxwell, D.S.O., a former Commanding Officer of the 1/8th Battalion, was appointed to the 174th Brigade.

On July 25th a daylight raid on a large scale was carried out, about 300 men going over the top. The raid met with little opposition on the front attacked, except in the neighbourhood of the Quarry, where some platoons of "A" Company had a very hard time. A few prisoners were brought back, and many more in attempting to escape had to be shot; but during the return journey the raiders received heavy machine-gun fire from the flanks of the attack, and suffered heavily. 2nd-Lieutenants Roft and Alexander were killed, and four officers wounded (2nd-Lieutenants Tafner, Scarth, Johnson, and Hatchett). Casualties to other ranks were 113. On the whole, it seems probable that the casualties on both sides were about equal. One remarkable feature was that the enemy allowed the wounded to be got in without interference. July 25th, 1918.

After a short rest at Round Wood, Franvillers (a place full of interest to those who had fought on the Somme in 1916), the Battalion moved to Baisieux, where they were joined by Lieutenant-Colonel Derviche-Jones, who had returned to take over the command of the Battalion from Lieutenant-Colonel Johnston, transferred to command the 7th Battalion.

Plans for the great counter-offensive which was to make history were kept very secret. On August 4th the Battalion was marched and entrained to a back area at Wargnies, near Canaples, and preparations made for a long period of rest and training there. Actually, with the exception of a few days at Neuf Moulin, no opportunity had been given to train the Battalion, a large number of whom consisted of youngsters hurriedly sent out as reinforcements to make good the gaps caused by the enemy offensive. These lads were soon to show their mettle, even without the advantage of training. On the night of August 4th the Battalion was moved by night from Wargnies, and, after entraining and marching, spent the day in a small copse on the Bray-Corbie road. A thick and continuous drizzle made things very uncomfortable, especially as the Battalion had to move up that night to relieve the 2nd Bedfords in the Sailly-Laurette Sector. A long march in the rain was followed by a long and BATTLE OF SOMME, August, 1918.

SAILLY-LAURETTE, August 6th, 1918.

difficult relief. The condition of communication and
front trenches was deplorable, and relief had not been
completed by dawn, when an assaulting Division of the
enemy, specially trained for the occasion, attacked the
18th Division front on the left and the two left companies
of this Battalion. These two companies (" A " and " D,"
under Captain Poulton and Lieutenant Wilkinson) put
up a most praiseworthy defence, and, in spite of the fact
that the Battalion on their left had been pushed back
more than 400 yards, maintained their front line intact
throughout, and, further, formed a defensive flank which
the enemy was unable to penetrate. Much assistance
was afforded by Lewis-gun fire from " B " Company
(Captain Thomas), which swept across the line of the
enemy attack and caused them numerous casualties.
Some prisoners and machine guns were also taken in a
bombing counter-attack initiated by 2nd-Lieutenant
Pattinson. The enemy, though foiled in their attempt
to pierce our lines, kept up an incessant bombardment of
the front-line system with 5·9's, gas shells, and trench
mortars. By the morning of the 8th, the date fixed for
the great counter-offensive, the men of this Battalion
were caked in mud from head to foot, had had practically
no rest (this was only possible by leaning against the
parados), and had repelled a determined attack by the
enemy.

MALARD WOOD, In order to keep the impending attack secret and jump
August 8th. a surprise on the enemy, instructions for the attack were
not issued until the morning of the 7th. The rôle of the
Battalion was to clear certain copses, and clear and hold
the west edge of Malard Wood. Actually this Battalion
was in reserve, but circumstances, in the form of a thick
mist limiting visibility to ten yards, thrust the Battalion
in the forefront of the fight a few minutes after the battle
commenced. The three days in the line, exciting and
tiring as they were, had given them a better idea of
direction than other troops could possibly have. The
luck of the weather was with them from the start, and
they were able to get right on top of the enemy before
the direction of the attack was perceived. Two enemy
Battalion Commanders and over 500 prisoners were taken
by the Battalion, as well as numerous trench mortars
and machine guns. The next day (9th) the Battalion
CHIPILLY, was attached to the 175th Brigade, and ordered to co-
August 9th. operate in an attack by the 174th Brigade on Chipilly
(which had given much trouble on the 8th), advancing
on the left flank of the Division astride the Bray-Corbie
road. An American Regiment participated on our right.
The attack, which was entirely open warfare, was successful. The casualties to this Battalion were far lighter

than the total number of unwounded prisoners taken. Officers killed: 2nd-Lieutenants Knell, Constance, Mason, and Captain Poulton; and seven wounded—Lieutenant-Colonel Derviche-Jones, Captains Barratt and Thomas, Lieutenant Wilkinson, 2nd-Lieutenants Perry and Crossland; and of other ranks about 290. It is noteworthy that all the officers on Battalion Headquarters were either killed or wounded.

Two days later the Battalion was relieved, and marched back to tents in Round Wood. Major Priestley was now in command, and directed the training of the Battalion until it moved on August 22nd to support an attack by the 18th Division on the Albert Sector, and, after concentrating at Morlancourt, the Battalion marched as part of the Brigade advance-guard to Billon Wood. The advance was extremely difficult, owing to an intensely dark night, a violent thunder-storm, incessant bombardments of gas shells and high explosives, and the fact that Major Priestley was badly wounded early in the operation. Captain Faber took over the command, and three companies—"A," "B" (Lieutenant Porter), and "D" (Lieutenant Newsome)—reached the wood about midnight. During the night "C" Company, who had lost touch, pushed through the wood, and all companies took part in the attack of the 26th. In spite of the greatest difficulties, objectives were taken and held. Major Henneker arrived about midnight to take the command, but was shortly afterwards wounded. Owing to the hurried move on the 25th, the Battalion had been compelled to march without water or rations, and owing to the incessant marching, fighting and shelling, and rain, remained without food until the night of the 27th-28th. The attack was renewed on the 27th and objectives taken, and again a further attack on the 28th enabled the line of the Perrone Road by Marrieres Wood to be captured and held. Some 150 prisoners were taken in these three attacks, and large numbers of machine guns, and also three field guns and forty enemy pigeons. Our casualties were: killed, two officers (Lieutenant Newsome and 2nd-Lieutenant Graham); five officers wounded (Major Priestley, Major Henneker, Captain Gunning, Lieutenant Humphreys, and 2nd-Lieutenant Orchard); other ranks, 186 killed and wounded.

BILLON WOOD, August 25th and 26th.

FARNEY WOOD, August 27th.

MARRIERES WOOD, August 28th.

After a day's rest and reorganization, the Brigade became advance guard, this Battalion forming the left half of the main guard, and proceeded past Hem Wood to a valley near Howitzer Wood. An early morning attack was ordered for the 31st, which was completely successful, though not without considerable casualties—two officers

HEM WOOD, August 31st.

killed (Captain Clarke, M.C., and 2nd-Lieutenant Rothwell) and five officers wounded (Lieutenant Porter and 2nd-Lieutenants Booth, Everett, L. J. Smith, and C. R. Smith). Casualties to other ranks, 105. Some 220 prisoners and numerous machine guns were captured by the Battalion.

HINDLEY WOOD. On September 1st, after six most arduous days' fighting, in which much important progress had been made, the Battalion was relieved and went to Hindley Wood. Here Major Wild (Royal West Kents) joined the Battalion and assumed command.

BATTLE OF EPEHY AND PEIZIERES. On September 6th the Battalion moved to Moislains, and thence to Ville Wood, and the next day a further move was made to Guyencourt, in order to attack the enemy at Epehy and Peizieres. On the 8th all four companies, under 2nd-Lieutenant Tallin, 2nd-Lieutenant Buck, 2nd-Lieutenant Youngman, and 2nd-Lieutenant Pattinson, advanced 1,000 yards without difficulty, when they came under heavy machine-gun fire, after capturing Wood Farm. Further progress was made, and parties of " D," " C," and " B " Companies entered the villages of Peizieres and Epehy. As no support was forthcoming on either flank, and the enemy was in far greater strength, these parties fell back to Tottenham Post, though some small groups remained in the villages until the next day. Great assistance was rendered by the 62nd Brigade R.F.A. (under Major Roney-Dougal), who advanced their guns to within 800 yards of the enemy. The Battalion was ordered to hold on at all cost, and did so until relieved on the 10th by the 12th Londons. Casualties from the 6th to the 10th : two officers killed (2nd-Lieutenants Fergusson and Riordan), four wounded (2nd-Lieutenants Youngman, Pattinson, Bassett, and Yale) ; other ranks, 141 killed and wounded.

LIERAMONT. After a few days spent quietly at Lieramont, the Battalion returned to the Epehy Sector for four days, and RONNSOY. afterwards to Ronnsoy, to help the 229th Brigade, relieving a Battalion of the Devons until the 24th, when the 105th American Regiment relieved this Battalion.

On the 27th Lieutenant-Colonel Grover took over the command, and the Battalion spent some days in moving, via Villers Faucon, Heilly, Château de la Haie, to Bully Grenay, in order to go into " peace trenches " at Loos. After the strenuous days of August and September, the Battalion was pretty thin, and looked forward to a period of comparative ease in stationary trenches.

The final stage of the war had now been entered upon. The Boches were being hammered on all sides, and, in fact, the great Boche retreat, only prevented by the Armistice from becoming a decisive rout, had already commenced. It was not surprising, therefore, to find that the Division would not be allowed to rest for any length of time. Almost immediately, on the 2nd, the Battalion advanced, and on the 4th an attack was made on the Cité St. Auguste, a suburb of Lens. This place was cleared by " D " Company (Lieutenant Anderson). " A " (Lieutenant Peters) and " D " Companies also secured the Railway Embankment and Coke Ovens, " B " Company (Captain Barratt) forming a protective screen to the advance. " A " and " C " Companies suffered severely from gas shells, the casualties being two officers wounded (Lieutenants Anderson and Hannah), and 94 other ranks. The next day an early attack was made on the Annay switch line, which was not quite so successful, owing to heavy trench-mortar and machine-gun fire.

FINAL PURSUIT. Loos, October, 1918.

LENS. Cité St. Auguste.

Annay.

After a brief spell of rest and training at Marqueffles' Farm, the Battalion moved to Montigny, and thence to Courrières, where the Battalion was directed to secure a bridgehead over the canal. Strong enemy opposition was encountered, and the remnants of two platoons of " D " Company (Captain Buck), after making a gallant fight, were captured on the canal bank. 2nd-Lieutenants Powl and Robinson were taken prisoners, and Lieutenant R. M. Kelly and 2nd-Lieutenant Benn were wounded. Casualties to other ranks, 89. During the night Lieutenant-Colonel Derviche-Jones, who had been commanding the 12th Londons for a few days, returned to the Battalion, vice Lieutenant-Colonel Grover, transferred to the 12th.

Courrières, October 14th.

The attack on the bridgehead was resumed on the 15th, and all objectives taken by mid-day (without casualties, in spite of opposition). At night outposts were established well the other side of the canal near Oignies, but patrols failed to find the enemy, who were retiring under the constant pressure from all sides.

Oignies, October 15th.

After a day's rest in Oignies, the Battalion made a night march to La Rushonette, and reached Mons-en-Pevelle at 6.30 a.m. Here they met with a rousing reception from the liberated inhabitants. The Battalion became the vanguard : " C " Company (Lieutenant Hallifax) on the right ; " B " Company (Captain Barratt) on the left of the main Bersee Road ; remaining companies— " A " (Lieutenant Humphreys) and " D " (Captain

Bersee, October 18th-19th.

Buck), with a Machine-Gun Company and Trench-Mortar Company—and a Battery of Artillery on the main road. Great difficulty was experienced in maintaining direction, owing to the wooded country and thick mists. Bersee was reached with little opposition, and the advance continued towards Wattines. On patrols reporting that the units of both flanks were halted some two miles in rear of our advanced positions, defensive flanks were thrown out, and the Battalion rested until the flank units could come up. In the meantime the enemy were putting up a strong resistance with machine guns and shells, and some casualties were suffered. After a sharp struggle, " B " Company entered and cleared Wattines at 2 a.m., and a line of outposts was placed outside the village. Again the inhabitants gave the Battalion a splendid reception. The 6th Londons became the vanguard the following day, and the 8th part of the main-guard, spending the night at Wattines Farm. Nomain was reached by the 6th Londons after a short preliminary encounter, and here the Brigade was rested for some days while the 175th Brigade advanced to the River Scheldt. Strenuous training in all forms of open advance and attack was carried out.

WATTINES, October 18th-19th.

NOMAIN, October 20th.

THE SCHELDT. RUE DOMBRIE.

The Battalion moved from Nomain on October 27th with battle transport, and relieved a unit of the 175th Brigade at Rue Dombrie. This place was vigorously shelled by the enemy, who were hanging on to the crossings of the Scheldt, and many casualties occurred. Subsequently the 7th Londons were relieved by this Battalion at Maulde, and outposts were held on the banks of the Scheldt. Various schemes were considered for crossing the network of rivers, canals, and floods here, and after a not altogether pleasant ten days, during which it was reported almost daily that the enemy had withdrawn (the receipt of such report being generally the signal for resumption of hostilities by the enemy), a general advance was ordered. After a difficult crossing on hastily improvised rafts, some made out of Boche cylinders and others of the bird-nest type, a crossing was effected at Montagne, and the last Boche outpost went flying. Outposts were established at Flines, and all fighting was practically over. Since the beginning of October there were but few days that this Battalion had not been under enemy fire. Marches were long, in all kinds of weather, and both by day or night. As soon as the region of inhabited houses was reached at Mons-en-Pevelle, the gratitude and hospitality of the people were unbounded, and did much to relieve the strain of the advance. On the Scheldt it was the British who had to evacuate the local inhabitants, owing to the con-

MAULDE.

FLINES, November 8th.

sistency with which the Boche shelled and gassed their villages. Everywhere bridges were systematically destroyed and vast craters blown in the roadways, especially at all cross-roads. The difficulties of transport were enormous, the work done by the sappers magnificent. Sections of sappers were with all vanguards, ready to start on the repair of roads and bridges with the least delay. For them work was continuous night and day.

On the 9th the advance was renewed, and the Canal D'Antoing crossed at Callenelle, where the Battalion slept —or rather worked on bridging—most of the night. An early morning start at daybreak, with a picnic breakfast at Brasmenil, where the transport caught up, was followed by a long march to Beloeil, where a halt was made for the night. CALLENELLE, November 9th.

BELOEIL, November 10th.

On the morning of the 11th, at dawn, a further advance was begun. Many rumours were flying about with regard to an impending Armistice. Nevertheless, all due precautions were taken. The 8th had the honour of being the vanguard on this day. Cyclist scouts were pushed out in front and on the flanks; cavalry were at hand to dash through if wanted. Everyone was in a state of subdued excitement when, about 10 a.m., Brigadier-General Maxwell and his Brigade Major (Captain McConnell, M.C.), with a cavalry escort, galloped up to the head of the Battalion, and informed the Colonel that the terms of the Armistice had been signed, and hostilities would cease at 11 a.m. The news was conveyed to the cheering troops by the Colonel, and confirmed by the compiler of these pages in a message written on the last page of the last Army Book 152 used by him in this war. WAUDIGNIES, November 11th. ARMISTICE DAY.

The scenes that day almost defy description. Scouts had conveyed the news to the neighbouring villages, where all manner of antiquated musical instruments were unearthed to welcome the British troops. Children strewed the roads with flowers; bouquets and garlands were thrown to the troops. Jugs of hot coffee and bumpers of wine were handed to officers and men as they passed. Flags were dragged out from hidden receptacles, and, amidst processions, speeches, and cheering, few escaped being hugged, while many were wept over, by the grateful Belgians. It was indeed a day of triumph, and one long to be remembered.

The last line of outposts of the Battalion was at Waudignies, with advanced posts at Bauffe, on the Mons-Ath road. In the course of a week a move was made to Beloeil, and thence to Peruwelz, where the Battalion stayed for three months until it was practically disembanded. PERUWELZ, November, 1918, to February, 1919.

bodied by demobilization and drafts for the Army of
Occupation. During these difficult days, when reaction
was inevitable and everybody had the natural desire to
get home, it is to their credit that the behaviour of the
London Territorials was exemplary throughout. Sports,
concerts, whist drives, dances, and race meetings helped
to pass the time, while the more serious duties of training,
education, and ceremonial were not neglected. The many
friendships formed with the good people of Peruwelz
will remain as more than a mere memory. In a tangible
form they are represented by the silk flag presented by
the Commune to Brigadier-General Maxwell. On opposite
page will be found the special order issued to the Battalion
on Armistice Day. It only remains now to say "Au
Revoir" to all the gallant comrades who have helped
the Post Office Rifles along their way to final victory,
and who have added so much lustre to the Regiment.
If these pages will serve to remind some of their struggles,
and to continue for all the spirit of loyalty and comradeship so magnificently displayed in the Great War, they
will have achieved their object.

V

SPECIAL ORDER

To Officers and Men of the 8th Battalion City of London Regiment (Post Office Rifles).

I WISH to congratulate the Battalion on the splendid spirit, courage, and endurance shown by all ranks, especially during the anxious days of the spring and early summer of this year, and the more stirring times of August, up to the 11th November —a day which will be for ever famous in history—and to thank all ranks for the consistent loyalty extended to me both personally and as Commander of the Battalion.

In 1917, when the 1/8th Battalion was magnificently upholding its name as a fine fighting unit, notably at Cambrai, the 2/8th was carving a great reputation for itself at Bullecourt and the Ypres Salient.

In 1918, after the amalgamation of the two Battalions, the fighting qualities of the 8th have been well proved during the enemy attacks at the Crozat Canal, Tergnier, Viry-Noreuil, Chauny, and Villers-Bretonneux, during the very strenuous fighting from Malard Wood to Epehy, and later in the pursuit of the enemy from Loos to Bauffe. The success which has always attended the efforts of this Battalion is due to the splendid co-operation between all ranks and to the indomitable spirit and devotion of each individual man.

I am indeed proud to have had command of such a splendid fighting force, and trust that the comradeship engendered by the War may endure during the years to come.

(Signed) A. D. DERVICHE-JONES,
Lieut.-Colonel,
Commanding 8th Battalion City of London Regiment
(Post Office Rifles).

IN THE FIELD,
November 11th, 1918.

VI

OFFICIAL SUMMARY OF CASUALTIES

A. 1/8TH BATTALION—

	Killed.		Wounded.		Missing.	
	Offrs.	O.R.	Offrs.	O.R.	Offrs.	O.R.
(a) From 17/3/15 to 31/12/15	8	117	11	425	—	—
(b) ,, 1/1/16 ,, 31/12/16	17	234	22	593	2	160
(c) ,, 1/1/17 ,, 31/1/18	7	182	19	528	1	26
Total	32	533	52	1546	3	186

B. 2/8TH BATTALION—

| From 26/1/17 to 31/1/18 | 7 | 220 | 29 | 675 | 6* | 134† |

C. 8TH BATTALION—

| From 1/2/18 to 11/11/18 | 14 | 274 | 46 | 1168 | 12‡ | 315§ |
| TOTAL | 53 | 1027 | 127 | 3389 | 21 | 635 |

	Officers.	Other Ranks.
Total—A.	87	2265
B.	42	1029
C.	72	1757
GRAND TOTAL	201	5051

NOTES—

* All these officers are presumed to be killed. None are known to have been prisoners.
† Over 100 killed, but not so reported officially.
‡ Six officers prisoners; others believed to be killed.
§ A considerable proportion of these were killed, but not so reported officially.

VII

HONOURS

This list, with one exception, includes only honours given to officers and other ranks while actually serving with the Post Office Rifles in France, and up to the New Year's Honours List of 1919.

V.C. (1).

370995 Sergt. Knight, A. J.

Extract from " London Gazette " of November 6th, 1917 :

For most conspicuous bravery and devotion to duty during the operations against the enemy positions.

Sergt. Knight did extraordinary good work, and showed exceptional bravery and initiative when his platoon was attacking an enemy strong point, and came under very heavy fire from an enemy machine gun. He rushed through our own barrage, bayonetted the enemy gunner, and captured the position single-handed.

Later, twelve of the enemy with a machine gun were encountered in a shell-hole. He again rushed forward by himself, bayoneted two and shot a third, and caused the remainder to scatter.

Subsequently, during the attack on a fortified farm, when entangled up to his waist in mud, and seeing a number of the enemy firing on our troops, he immediately opened fire on them without waiting to extricate himself from the mud, killing six of the enemy.

Again, noticing the company on his right flank being held up in their attack on another farm, Sergt. Knight collected some men and took up a position on the flank of this farm, from where he brought a heavy fire to bear on the farm, as a result of which the farm was captured.

All platoon officers of the company had become casualties before the first objective was reached, and this gallant N.C.O. took command of all the men of his platoon and of the platoons without officers. His energy in consolidating and reorganizing was untiring.

His several single-handed actions showed exceptional bravery, and saved a great number of casualties in the company. They were performed under heavy machine-gun and rifle fire, and without regard to personal risk, and were the direct cause of the objectives being captured.

C.M.G. (1).
Brig.-Gen. A. Maxwell.

Bar to D.S.O. (2).
Brig.-Gen. A. Maxwell.   Lieut.-Col. A. D. Derviche-Jones.

D.S.O. (5).
Brig.-Gen. A. Maxwell.   Lieut.-Col. A. D. Derviche-Jones.
Lieut.-Col. J. Harvey.   Lieut.-Col. W. B. Vince.
Major W. J. Whitehead.

Bar to M.C. (5).
Major A. C. Soutten.   Capt. C. Kelly.
Capt. G. E. Gunning.   Capt. A. S. Thomas.
Lieut. W. H. Richardson.

M.C. (36).
Lt.-Col. C. E. Johnston.
Lt.-Col. W. B. Vince.
Major H. W. Priestley.
Capt. A. C. Alexander.
Capt. T. Boss.
Capt. H. Booth.
Capt. E. C. K. Clarke.
Capt. E. B. Davies.
Capt. F. Deverill.
Capt. and Qr.-Mr. R. Fairley.
Capt. G. E. Gunning.
Capt. A. D. Heaton.
Capt. C. Kelly.
Capt. E. R. Lanes.
Capt. H. Massy-Miles, R.A.M.C.
Capt. Mitchell.
Capt. T. J. Mumford.
Capt. Home Peel.
Capt. C. Perry, C.F.
Capt. A. S. Thomas.
Capt. L. T. Whelan, R.A.M.C.
Lt. W. H. Richardson.
Lt. T. W. Porter.
2nd-Lt. C. S. Armstrong.
2nd-Lt. J. M. Barratt.
2nd-Lt. G. W. Chancellor.
2nd-Lt. C. R. Crossland.
2nd-Lt. E. C. Knell.
2nd-Lt. E. M. Lewis.
2nd-Lt. R. B. Pattinson.
2nd-Lt. W. B. Scarth.
2nd-Lt. L. J. Smith.
2nd-Lt. W. J. Ward.
2nd-Lt. W. Will.
1443 C.S.M. Chivers, M. C.
370501 C.S.M. Turner, H. M.

Bar to D.C.M. (2).
370506 Sgt. Mattock, C. A.   370680 A./C.S.M. Windle, W.

D.C.M. (24).

52067 L./Cpl. Blake, W.
373704 L./Cpl. Davies, J. G.
300515 Sgt. Dare, E. C.
370719 Sgt. Fernee, H.
370625 Sgt. Francis, H. J.
370744 Sgt. Harris, G. H.
370172 Sgt. Heather, W. A. G.
371540 Sgt. Horrocks, C. E.
371265 Rfn. McClosky, E.
372639 Sgt. McIntosh, A.
370506 Sgt. Mattock, C. A.
370470 Sgt. Morrel, F.
371575 Sgt. Payne, H.
370041 C.S.M. Peat, R. J
374135 Rfn. Randell, E. L.
370451 Sgt. Rushforth, C. H.
370265 Sgt. Rushforth, S. W.
370390 Sgt. Simpson, W.
370013 C.S.M. Stanton, W. A.
371610 Rfn. Tyrell, F. G.
2026 L./Cpl. Varney, W. J.
370680 A./C.S.M. Windle, W.
634 A./R.S.M. Witheridge, P.
372612 Sgt. Yardley, W.

Bar to M.M. (7).

371540 Sgt. Horrocks, C. E.
370646 Sgt. Nunn, J. T.
371311 L./Cpl. Solomon, G.
373104 Sgt. Tassart, A.
370419 L./Sgt. Carroll, S. J.
371116 Rfn. Griffiths, A. C.
370772 Sgt. Hayward, C. R.

M.M. (153).

202030 Rfn. Adeoni, J.
370327 L./Sgt. Andrews, J. L.
371244 Rfn. Armstrong, H.
375037 Rfn. Adlam, T.
372756 Sgt. Antram, A. E.
374867 Rfn. Allen, W. C.
370391 L./Cpl. Barber, H. S.
201790 L./Cpl. Barnes, J.
372585 Rfn. Barron, A.
372746 Cpl. Bailey, W. C.
370418 A./Cpl. Ballantyne, W.
46300 Rfn. Baddams, H. J.
372434 Rfn. Bacon, W. A.
371291 L./Sgt. Baldock, W. T.
372491 Rfn. Bass, C. H. C.
371206 Rfn. Barker, H.
372258 A./Cpl. Bear, H. D.
370034 Sgt. Bell, G.
370164 Sgt. Bliss, W. C.
371593 Cpl. Board, J. E.
2496 Cpl. Bodley, J. H.
370589 Rfn. Bowman, C. J.
370051 R.Q.M.S. Brand, E. L.
385156 Rfn. Bray, T. V.
370243 Cpl. Brockwell, A. P.
370419 L./Sgt. Carroll, S. J.
375408 Rfn. Carstairs, G.
371357 L./Cpl. Clayton, R. W.
40490 Rfn. Coggons, G.
373861 Cpl. Condon, G. W
371682 L./Cpl. Cook, T.
372983 Rfn. Cripps, P. J.
372343 L./Cpl. Crowe, F. D.
375584 Rfn. Dalziel, W. G.
370334 Rfn. Dixon, A. W.
370617 Sgt. Dixon, C. R.

M.M.—*Continued.*

372617 Rfn. Dixon, W. A.
371043 Sgt. Dogherty, P.
370747 Rfn. Drew, H. J.
373116 Rfn. Ebbs, W.
372114 Rfn. Edwards, H. C.
372660 L./Cpl. Elkins, J.
374254 Rfn. Elsey, W. G.
3419 L./Cpl. Evans, E.
372011 Rfn. Evans, R. D.
373283 Cpl. Featherstone, W.
370231 L./Sgt. Fenwick, A. V.
370061 Sgt. Fisher, J. H.
371391 Sgt. Flynn, C. J.
372955 Rfn. Forrest, R.
371955 A./Sgt. Foxall, A. L.
1413 Sgt. Fry, T. J.
370604 Rfn. Gandell, W. E.
370073 Sgt. Gatting, C. A.
371397 Cpl. Gibbs, T. M.
370862 L./Cpl. Grant, F. J.
301633 Rfn. Gray, A.
371116 Rfn. Griffiths, A. C.
372661 L./Cpl. Hall, J. A.
375551 Rfn. Hall, W. J.
371295 Rfn. Hands, E.
373431 A./C.S.M. Hawkins, E. C.
370411 L./Sgt. Hayes, J. J.
370688 Cpl. Hayes, H. J.
372698 L./Cpl. Hellings, S.
370772 Sgt. Hayward, C. R.
370437 A./Sgt. Hilling, J. A.
302727 L./Sgt. Hodges, H. W.
371970 Rfn. Hollingsworth, F.
370184 Rfn. Howard, W. T.
371540 Sgt. Horrocks, C. E.
372654 Rfn. Jefferson, C. W.
370319 Rfn. Jenner, J. H.
370417 Cpl. Jeffery, J. P.

372174 Rfn. Johnson, S. E.
370029 Rfn. Kattan, H. A. V.
370422 L./Cpl. Knibb, W. B.
370499 Cpl. Kramer, G.
370566 Sgt. Lawler, A. H.
371219 A./Cpl. Lowry, W.
370898 Sgt. Lambkin, W. A.
370913 Sgt. Lamming, A. H.
4237 Rfn. Lane, A. R.
371164 Rfn. McIntyre, A. T.
372512 Cpl. McKenzie, F.
372548 A./Sgt. Mitchley, B. A. F.
372301 A./Cpl. Murphy, M.
370979 Sgt. Murray, B. T.
374342 Rfn. Markham, C. A.
370151 Sgt. Martin, A. J.
371123 Rfn. Moyne, R.
370487 L./Cpl. Moxey, G. S.
371243 L./Cpl. McDermott, M. J.
371014 A./Cpl. Miskelly, H.
13202 L./Cpl. Manning, J. A.
373969 Sgt. Molland, H. J.
376233 Rfn. Murray, W. R.
370690 Rfn. Millington, R.
52059 Rfn. Martin, H. G.
370646 Sgt. Nunn, J. T.
371360 A./Cpl. Needley, F.
374038 Rfn. Nicholls, J.
370724 Rfn. Plummer, P. G.
372631 L./Cpl. Payne, E.
370494 L./Cpl. Pemberton, H. W.
371217 Sgt. Plant, A. E. B.
370347 L./Cpl. Price, J H.
370303 Rfn. Pollard, J. E.
370369 L./Cpl. Patston, H. R.
372474 Rfn. Roper, F. V.

M.M.—*Continued.*

371653 Rfn. Robeson, A.
374074 Rfn. Raynor, J. B.
370368 Cpl. Richbell, J. J.
370997 L./Cpl. Revell, B.
375093 Rfn. Richardson, E. G.
371053 L./Cpl. Reynolds, G. W.
370099 L./Sgt. Rhodes, A.
370673 L./Sgt. Seager, G. A.
372609 Rfn. Soper, J.
372866 Rfn. Sprakes, E.
371002 Sgt. Salt, W. H.
371503 Sgt. Small, J. A.
371311 L./Cpl. Solomon, G.
370750 L./Cpl. Staig, A. J.
372251 L./Sgt. Spear, B. H.
373462 Rfn. Spence, W.
375772 Rfn. Smith, W.
372808 Rfn. Stimson, A. E.
372532 Cpl. Staton, A.
370248 Cpl. Simons, F.
375955 Rfn. Sitch, G. W.
372506 L./Cpl. Stokes, A. F.
S/6953 Rfn. Sparkes, F.
373104 Sgt. Tassart, A.
385057 L./Sgt. Todd, A.
370380 Cpl. Taylor, J. E.
372384 L./Cpl. Turnbull, T.
370291 L./Cpl. Tillson, E. F.
370479 Rfn. Tait, R. A.
33589 Rfn. Tomkins, L. W.
2026 L./Cpl. Varney, W. J.
302002 L./Cpl. Vauzelles, S. E.
385155 Rfn. White, A. R.
372547 Rfn. Wright, W. A.
371543 Rfn. Watson, W. J.
371821 Rfn. Weekes, F. J.
371020 Rfn. Waterston, A.
374807 Rfn. Wilkinson, E.
374512 Rfn. Winfield, W.
370124 Rfn. Young, W. E.
370478 Sgt. Young, E. N.
376064 Rfn. Young, W.
3774 L./Cpl. Yelland, R. H.

M.S.M. (8).

370133 R.Q.M.S. Carnon, F. W.
370308 Rfn. Chelin, T.
371020 Sgt. Collins, D.
370436 C.Q.M.S. Harris, C.
370746 R.Q.M.S. Newman, F.A.
371753 Sgt. Penwarden, S. H.
370561 Sgt. Phillipps, C. E.
370257 Sgt. Skingsley, A. M.

1st Class Croix de Guerre (1).
370536 C.Q.M.S. Bianchi, F. W.

Belgian Croix de Guerre (2).
370133 R.Q.M.S. Carnon, F. W.   2199 A./R.S.M. Swain, T. E.

Dec. Militaire (1).
370807 Sgt. Blick, H. J.

With about 25 mentioned in dispatches and several parchment certificates for gallantry.

www.ingramcontent.com/pod-product-compliance
Lightning Source LLC
Chambersburg PA
CBHW060222050426
42446CB00013B/3140